HAPPY HOUR

A Drink For Every Moment Of Fun

J. L. Scott – "The Cocktailist"

Cover artwork by Freepic.com

Dinner party –

- Summer BBQ's

OR...just because!

Tired of drinking those same ole drinks?
Me too!
Well let's shake things up a bit.

Introducing my unique but tasty line of drinks, great for all adult parties with family/friends, private events or simply for self-indulgence.

In my Happy Hour book you'll find a list of amazing discoveries through trial and mix. I just know you will enjoy it.

CHEERS!

Happy Hour necessities:

- Metal 28oz shaker
- Strainer
- Ice Tongs
- Two side stainless steel jigger (shot glass)
- Stir spoon
- Martini glasses
- Highball glasses
- Old fashion glass
- Mason jar glass

LET'S GET TIPSY!

A Lady As Usual
2oz   Coconut Rum
1oz   Peach Schnapps
½oz   Jamaican Rum
½oz   Melon Liqueur
Mix in shaker
Pour into highball glass
Float Orange Juice on Top

All About Me
2oz Vodka
1oz Coconut Rum
1oz Amaretto
1oz Apple Puckers
Fill with Cranberry Juice
Mix in shaker
Pour into martini glass

A Smile On My Face
1oz 100 proof whiskey liqueur
1oz Amaretto
1oz Coconut Rum
Fill with Orange Juice
Mix in shaker
Pour into highball glass
Top with grenadine

Addictive
2oz Vodka
1oz Limon Rum
1oz Apple Pucker
1oz Peach schnapps
Fill with Orange Juice
Pour into highball glass
Top with grenadine

A Kick In The Ass
1oz Light Rum
1oz Orange flavor rum
1oz Jamaican Rum
Fill with Cranberry Juice
Mix in shaker
Pour in martini glass
Top off with Amaretto

As High As a Kite
2oz Vodka
2oz Coconut Rum
1oz Melon Liqueur
Fill with Cranberry Juice
Mix in shaker
Pour into martini glass

Ambition
2oz Vodka
2oz Light Rum
½ oz Coconut Rum
½ oz Amaretto
½ oz Whiskey liqueur
½ oz Peach Schnapps
½ oz Triple Sec
Fill with Orange juice or Cranberry Juice
Mix in shaker
Pour into highball glass

Beautiful
½ oz Vodka
1oz Coconut Rum
1oz Peach Schnapps
1oz Strawberry Schnapps
fill with Cranberry Juice
Mix in shaker
Pour in martini glass

Blow Your Horn
2oz Vodka
1oz Strawberry Rum
1oz Strawberry Schnapps
1oz Triple Sec
Splash of Limoncello
Fill with Orange Juice
Mix in shaker
Pour into highball glass

Body Heat
1oz Jamaican rum
½ oz Whiskey Liqueur
1oz Amaretto
1oz Light rum
Fill with Orange Juice or Cranberry Juice
Mix in shaker
Pour into old fashion glass
Drop a few Red hot candy in the bottom of glass

Bail Out
2oz Amaretto
1oz 1oo proof Whiskey Liqueur
1oz Dark rum
Fill with Cranberry Juice
Mix in shaker
Pour into old fashion glass
Top off with coconut rum

Blank Stare
2oz Light rum
1oz Orange rum
1oz Mango rum
1oz Coconut Rum
Fill with Cranberry juice
Mix in shaker
Pour into martini glass

Classic Moment
2oz Moscato
2oz Riesling
2oz Peach Schnapps
1oz Triple sec
fill with Orange juice
Stir in shaker
Pour into highball glass
Top off with Prosecco

Crystal Clear
2oz Light rum
1oz Peach rum
1oz Peach Schnapps
Fill with White cranberry peach juice
Mix in shaker
Pour into martini glass

Caution
1oz Light rum
1oz Apple rum
1oz Peach rum
1oz Strawberry Rum
1oz Limon rum
Fill with Cranberry juice and Pineapple juice
Mix in shaker
Pour into highball glass

Call Me Sunshine
2oz Light rum
1oz Strawberry rum
1oz Peach rum
Fill with Orange Juice
Mix in shaker
Pour in highball glass

Cotton Candy
2oz Vodka
1oz Coconut Tequila
1oz Mango Schnapps
1oz Blue curacao
Fill with White cranberry peach juice
Mix in shaker
Pour into martini glass

Cold Hearted Bastard
1oz Dark rum 151 proof
½ oz Amaretto
½ oz Whiskey liqueur
Fill with Orange Juice and Pineapple Juice or just
Orange Juice
Mix in shaker
Pour into old fashion glass

Deny
2oz Vodka
2oz Melon liqueur
1oz Mango Schnapps
1oz Coconut Rum
Fill with Orange Juice
Mix in shaker
Pour in martini glass

Damn That Was Good
2oz Amaretto
1oz Peach Schnapps
1oz Banana Schnapps
Splash of Gin
Fill with Fruit Punch
Mix in shaker
Pour into old fashion glass

Dirty Thoughts
2oz Whiskey Liqueur
1oz Amaretto
1oz Peach schnapps
1oz Coconut rum
1oz Triple Sec
Fill with Cranberry Juice
Mix in shaker
Pour into highball glass

Dangerous
2oz Amaretto
2oz Orange rum
Fill with Orange Juice
Top off with a splash of Dark rum
Mix in shaker
Pour into old fashion glass

Daydreaming
2oz Vodka
1oz Apple puckers
1oz Mango puckers
Fill with Orange Juice or White cranberry peach juice
Mix in shaker
Pour into martini glass

Dip It Low

2oz Light rum
1oz Berry fusion schnapps
1oz Triple sec
Fill with Orange Juice and White cranberry peach juice
Mix in shaker
Pour into martini glass

Deep Blue Sea

2oz Pineapple Vodka
2oz Berry fusion schnapps
1oz Blue curacao
Fill with Pineapple Juice
Mix in shaker
Pour into highball glass

Economic Relief

1oz Black cherry Vodka
1oz Coconut tequila
1oz Cherry schnapps
fill with Pineapple Juice or Cranberry Juice
Mix in shaker
Pour in old fashion glass

Enjoy Yourself
2oz Vodka
1oz Cherry Brandy
1oz Strawberry schnapps
Fill with Pineapple Juice
Mix in shaker
Pour into martini glass

Essence
½ oz Vodka
½ oz Mango Rum
½ oz Peach Schnapps
½ oz Strawberry Schnapps
½ oz Banana Schnapps
½ oz Apple Puckers
Fill with Pineapple juice
Mix in shaker
Pour into highball glass

Elite
1oz Whiskey liqueur
1oz Coconut rum
1oz Vanilla rum
Fill with Orange Juice
Stir in shaker
Pour into old fashion glass

Ease My Mind
2oz Vodka
1oz Triple sec
1oz Apple Puckers
1oz Lime Juice
Mix in shaker
Pour into martini glass
1oz Simple Syrup
Fill with Ginger Beer

Easy on The Eyes
2oz Vodka
1oz Grape puckers
1oz Mango puckers
Fill with White cranberry peach juice
Mix in shaker
Pour into highball glass

Filthy Water
1oz Vodka
1oz Grape Puckers
1oz Mango
1oz Amaretto
Fill with Orange Juice
Mix in shaker
Pour into highball glass

Fancy Free
1oz Vodka
1oz Watermelon Puckers
2oz Mango Puckers
1oz Orange juice
1oz Lemonade
Mix in shaker
Pour into highball glass

Fruit Cocktail
½ oz Peach Rum
½ oz Strawberry Rum
½ oz Pomegranate puckers
½ oz Watermelon Puckers
2oz Lemonade
2oz Raspberry lemonade
Fill with Orange Juice
Mix in shaker
Pour into highball glass
Add a splash of Amaretto

Forget Me Not
2oz Gala Apple vodka
1oz Coconut rum
1oz Mango Schnapps
Fill with Cranberry Juice
Mix in shaker
Pour into martini glass

Final Kahl
2oz Orange Rum
2oz Melon Rum
Fill with Orange Juice
Mix in shaker
Pour into martini glass

Forbidden Fruit
1oz Light rum
1oz Peach schnapps
1oz Cherry Schnapps
Fill with Orange Juice
Mix in shaker
Pour into martini glass

Fortune Teller
Wipe rim of glass with a slice of lemon and then roll
the rim in sugar
1oz Tequila
½ oz Strawberry Rum
½ oz Pomegranate schnapps
Fill with Lemonade
Mix in shaker
Pour into martini glass

Femme Fatale

1oz Light rum
1oz Melon rum
1oz Watermelon puckers
Splash of Cranberry Juice
Mix in shaker
Pour into old fashion glass

Fade to Black

1oz Apple Rum
1oz Strawberry rum
2oz Apple puckers
Fill with Peach Ice tea
Mix in shaker
Pour into highball glass
Then add ½ oz of Grenadine
Top off with Blueberry puckers

Green Expectations

2oz vodka
2oz Blue Curacao
2oz Amaretto
1oz Pineapple juice
1oz Orange juice
Mix in shaker
Pour into highball glass

Girls Nite
1oz Orange rum
1oz Strawberry puckers
3oz Grape juice
Mix in shaker
Pour into martini glass

Great Scott
1oz vodka
½ oz Banana Schnapps
½ oz Island Puckers
½ oz Blue Curacao
Fill with Orange Juice
Mix in shaker
Pour into highball glass

Glorious Moment
1oz Peach vodka
1oz Strawberry puckers
Splash of Amaretto
Splash of Whiskey Liqueur
Fill with Orange Juice
Mix in shaker
Pour into old fashion glass

Give Me Strength
1oz Whiskey liqueur
1oz Jamaican rum
1oz Colada Vodka
1oz Peach Schnapps
1oz Orange juice
1oz Pineapple juice
1oz Apple Juice
Mix in shaker
Pour into highball glass

Good Girl
Put a few Strawberries in the shaker
1oz Whiskey liqueur
1oz Jamaican rum
1oz Strawberry puckers
Fill with Orange Juice and Cranberry Juice
Mix in shaker
Pour in martini glass

Grown Ass Woman
1oz Whipped Vodka
1oz Whiskey liqueur
1oz Amaretto
1oz Triple Sec
Mix in shaker
Pour into old fashion glass

Guilty Pleasure
2oz Pear vodka
2oz Triple Sec
Fill with lemonade
Mix in shaker
Pour into martini glass

Happy Days
1oz Whipped Vodka
½ oz Mango schnapps
½ oz Strawberry Schnapps
Fill with Fruit punch
Mix in shaker
Pour into martini glass

How Did I Get Here
½ oz Vodka
½ oz Gin
½ oz Limon rum
½ oz Orange rum
Dash of Amaretto
Dash of Sweet and Sour mix
Stir in shaker
Pour into old fashion glass

I'm F#kd Up
1oz Vodka
1oz light rum
1oz tequila
1oz peach rum
1oz Triple sec
Fill with White Cranberry peach juice or Cranberry juice
Mix in shaker
Pour into highball glass

Imagine
1oz Pineapple vodka
1oz Limon rum
1oz Triple sec
2oz Peach juice (from canned peaches)
Fill with Fruit Punch
Mix in shaker
Pour into highball glass

Junk
1oz Black cherry Vodka
½ oz White Crème De Cacao
½ oz Cherry puckers
½ oz Berry infused puckers
½ oz peach puckers
Fill with Orange Juice and Cranberry Juice
Mix in shaker
Pour into highball glass
Float Amaretto on top

Just Because
1oz Pomegranate vodka
1oz Citron vodka
1oz Pomegranate Schnapps
Fill with Pomegranate Juice
Mix in shaker
Pour into martini glass

Laid Back
2oz Coconut rum tequila
1oz Coconut Vodka
Fill with Orange Juice
Mix in shaker
Pour into martini glass
Float Amaretto on top

My Kind of Apple
1oz Gala Apple Vodka
1oz Apple puckers
1oz Mango Rum
Fill with Cranberry apple juice
Mix in shaker
Pour into highball glass

Magnificent
1oz Vodka
1oz Grapefruit rum
1oz Coconut Vodka
Mix in shaker
Pour into martini glass
Float Rose' champagne on top

Mixed Emotions
Fill glass with ice
2oz Coconut rum
2oz Amaretto
2oz Peach puckers
Mix in shaker
Pour into highball glass
Slowly pour lemonade into glass until glass is full

Notorious
Wipe rim of glass with a slice of lemon and then roll rim in sugar
1oz Orange rum
1oz Coconut rum
1oz Mango schnapps
1oz Lemon juice
Mix into shaker
Pour into martini glass

Pot Of Gold
1oz Banana Schnapps
1oz Light rum
1oz Triple Sec
Fill with Orange Juice
Mix in shaker
Pour into highball glass

Purple Thoughts
1oz Vodka
1oz Apple vodka
1oz Pineapple Rum
1oz Berry Fusion
Fill with Cranberry juice
Mix in shake
Pour into highball glass

Purple Velvet
2oz Limon Rum
1oz Island Puckers
Fill with Cranberry Juice
Mix in shaker
Pour into martini

Surprise Witness
1oz Light Rum
1oz Apple Puckers
1oz Triple Sec
Fill with Cranberry juice
Mix in shaker
Pour into highball glass

Science Project
1oz Light Rum
1oz Peach rum
1oz Melon Liqueur
Fill with Orange Juice
Mix in shaker
Pour into highball glass

See Through
1oz Light Rum
1oz Apple rum
1oz Limon rum
1oz Triple sec
Fill White Cranberry peach juice
Mix in shaker
Pour into martini glass

Some Kind Of Wonderful
1oz Limoncello
1oz Limon rum
1oz Triple sec
Mix in shaker
Pour into martini glass
Float Cranberry juice on top

Southern Joy
2oz Black cherry Vodka
1oz Peach schnapps
1oz Watermelon schnapps
1oz Triple sec
Fill with Mango peach juice
Mix in shaker
Pour into mason jar

Satisfaction
1oz Vodka
1oz Whipped vodka
1oz Coconut vodka
Fill with Cranberry juice
Mix in shaker
Pour into martini glass
Float Watermelon pucker on top

Sittin In the Clouds
2oz Amaretto
2oz Jamaican Rum
2oz Whiskey Liqueur
Fill with Orange Juice
Mix in shaker
Pour into old fashion glass

Transparent
Rub a slice of lemon on the rim of glass and then rub
rim of glass in sugar
1oz Strawberry rum
1oz Coconut rum
1oz Triple sec
Mix in shaker
Pour into martini glass
Add a splash of Lemonade

Two Face

½ oz Vodka
½ oz Peach rum
½ oz Apple rum
½ oz Coconut rum
½ oz Triple sec
½ oz Blue Curacao
Mix in shaker
Pour into highball glass
Pour Orange Juice slowly in the glass

Taste The Rainbow

½ oz Orange rum
½ oz Strawberry rum
½ oz Limon rum
½ oz Watermelon rum
½ oz Mango schnapps
Fill with White cranberry peach juice
Mix in shaker
Pour into highball glass

NOTES

Made in the USA
Las Vegas, NV
27 May 2021